SCHIRMER'S LIBRARY
OF MUSICAL CLASSICS

Vol. 2090

Henry Schradieck

The School of Violin Technics
Complete
Books 1-3 and Complete Scale Studies

ISBN 978-1-4234-9089-0

G. SCHIRMER, Inc.

DISTRIBUTED BY

HAL•LEONARD®
CORPORATION
7777 W. BLUEMOUND RD. P.O. BOX 13819 MILWAUKEE, WI 53213

www.schirmer.com
www.halleonard.com

CONTENTS

The School of Violin-Technics, Book I
(Exercises for Promoting Dexterity in the Various Positions)

The School of Violin-Technics, Book II (Exercises in Double-stops)

The School of Violin-Technics, Book III (Exercises in Various Bowings)

Complete Scale-Studies

The School of Violin-Technics
Book I
Exercises for Promoting Dexterity in the Various Positions

Henry Schradieck
(1846–1918)

I. Exercises on One String

The pupil should be careful in all the exercises to keep the hand perfectly quiet, letting the fingers fall strongly, and raising them with elasticity.

The tempo must be lessened or accelerated, according to the ability of the pupil, but is generally moderate.

II.

III. Exercises on Two Strings

IV. Exercises to be practiced with wrist-movement only, keeping the right arm perfectly quiet

V. Exercises on Three Strings

VI. Exercises on Four Strings

VII. Exercises on Four Strings

VIII. Exercises in the Second Position

IX. Exercises in the First and Second Positions

15

X. Exercises in the Third Position

XI. Exercises in the First, Second and Third Positions

19

XII. Exercises in the Fourth Position

XIII. Exercises on the First, Second, Third and Fourth Positions

XIV. Exercises in the Fifth Position

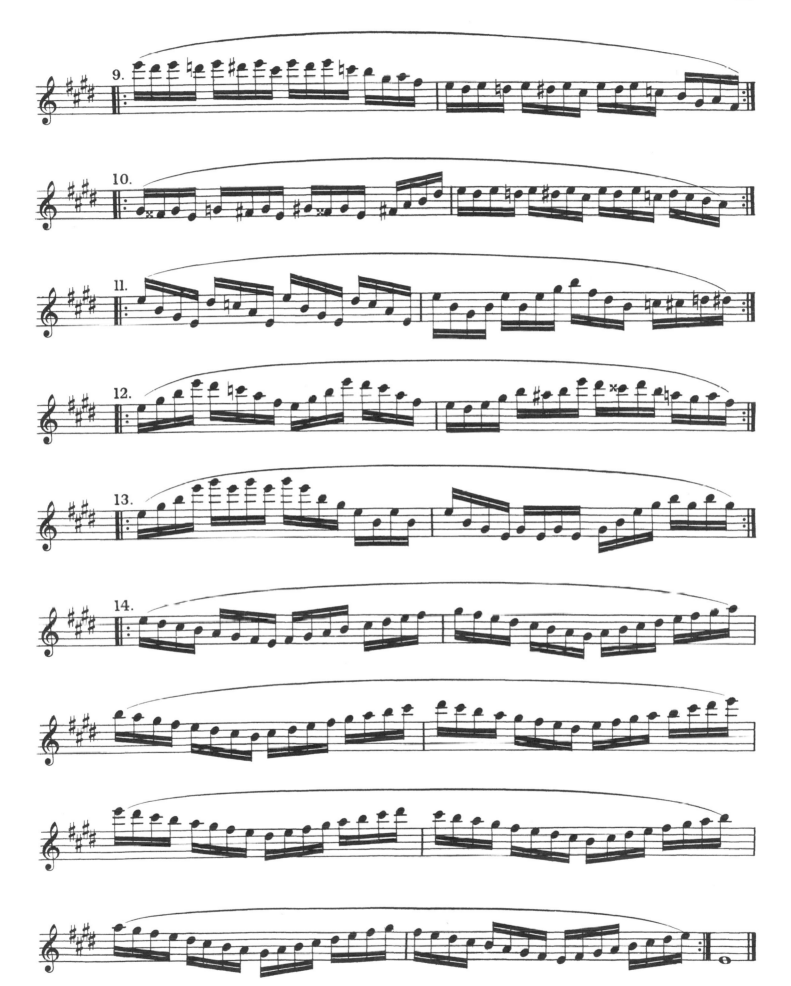

25

XV. Exercises passing through Five Positions

XVI. Exercises in the Sixth Position

XVII. Exercises passing through Six Positions

31

XVII. Exercises in the Seventh Position

XIX.

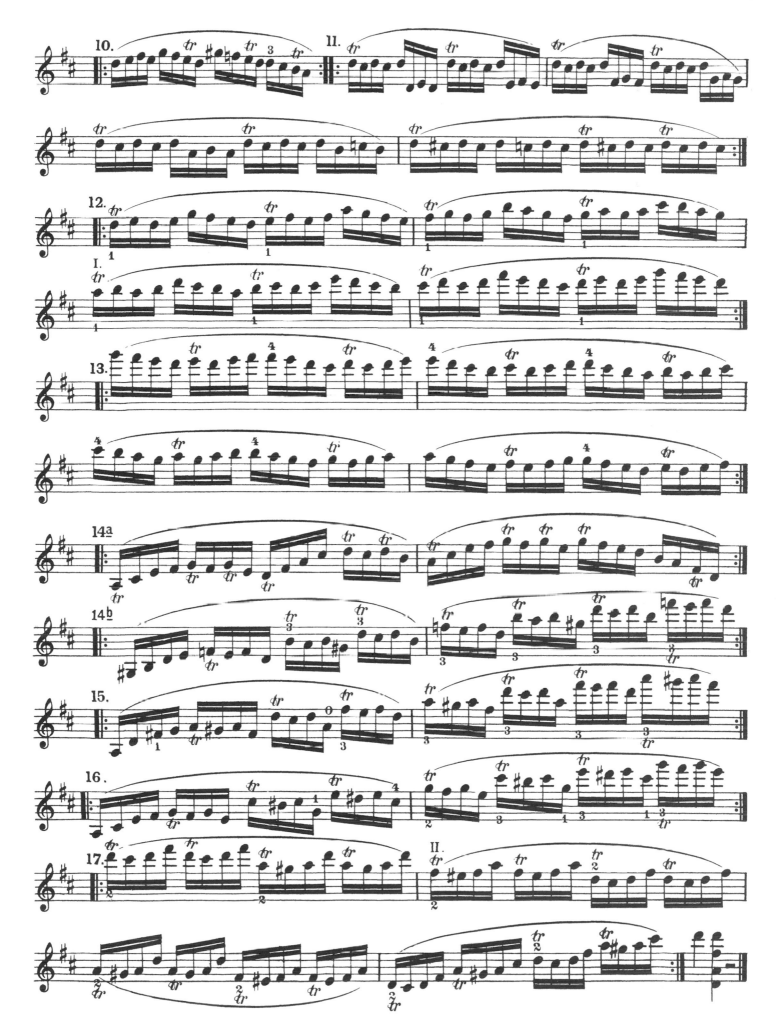

35

XX.

40

14. Allegro vivace.

15. Energico.

44

46

47

remain

at the nut

48

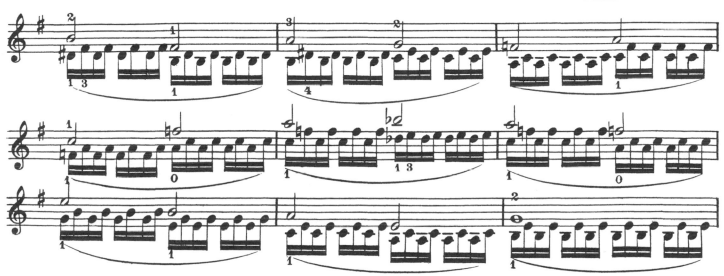

(This page has intentionally been left blank.)

The School of Violin-Technics
Book II
Exercises in Double-stops

Henry Schradieck
(1846–1918)

I.

II.

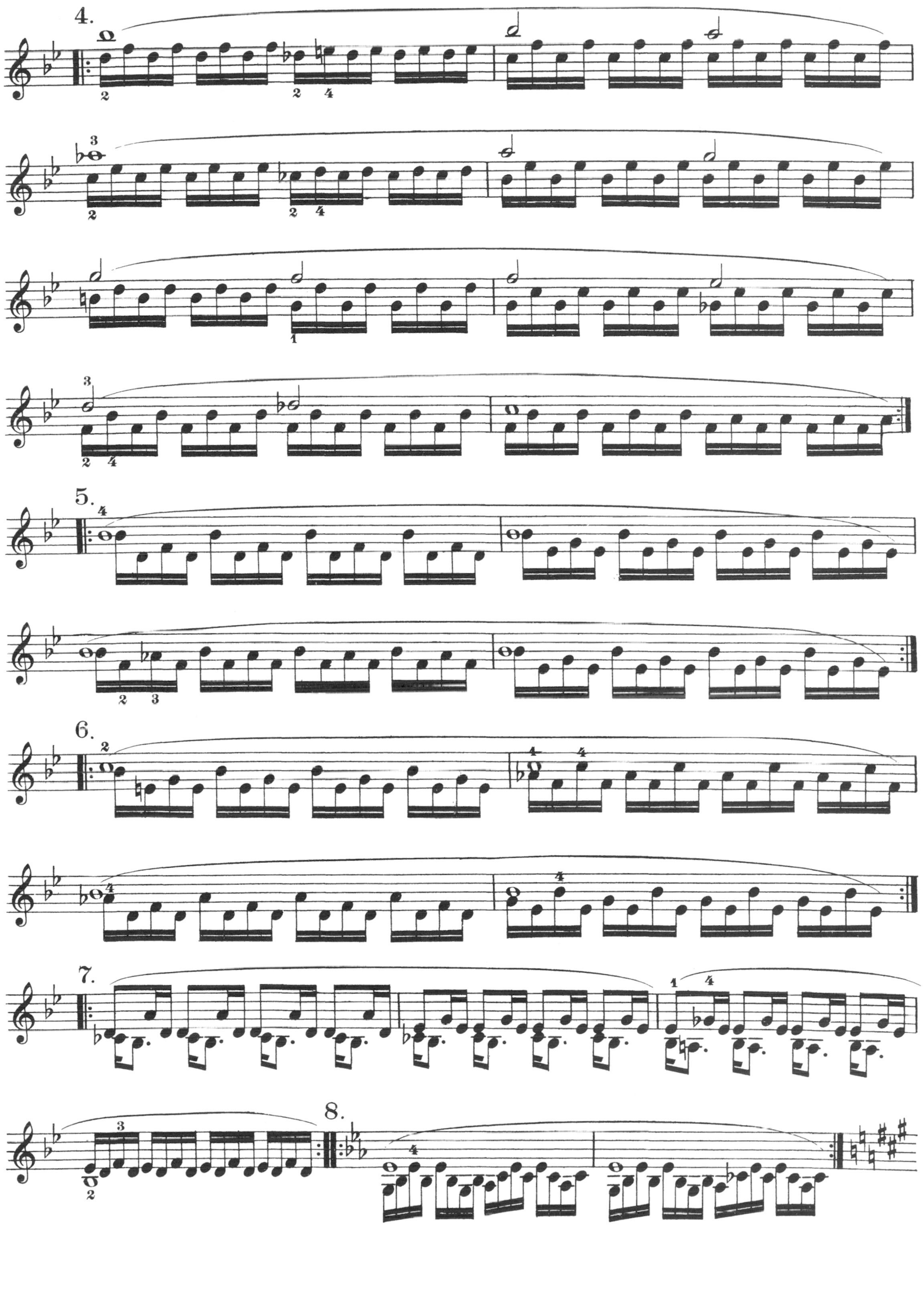
4.
5.
6.
7.
8.

56

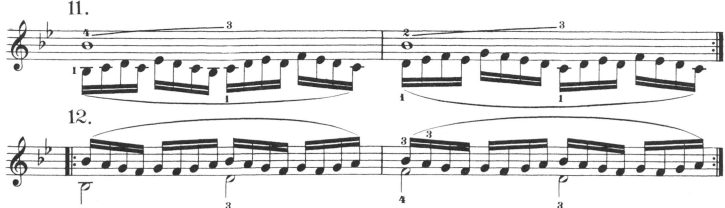

III.

IV.

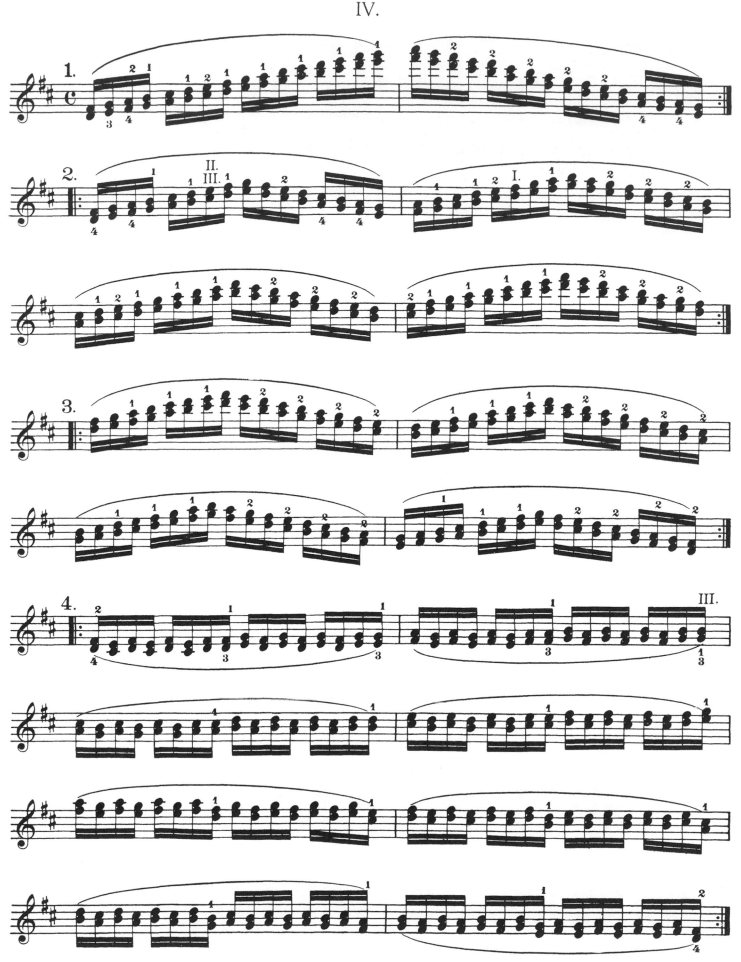

V.

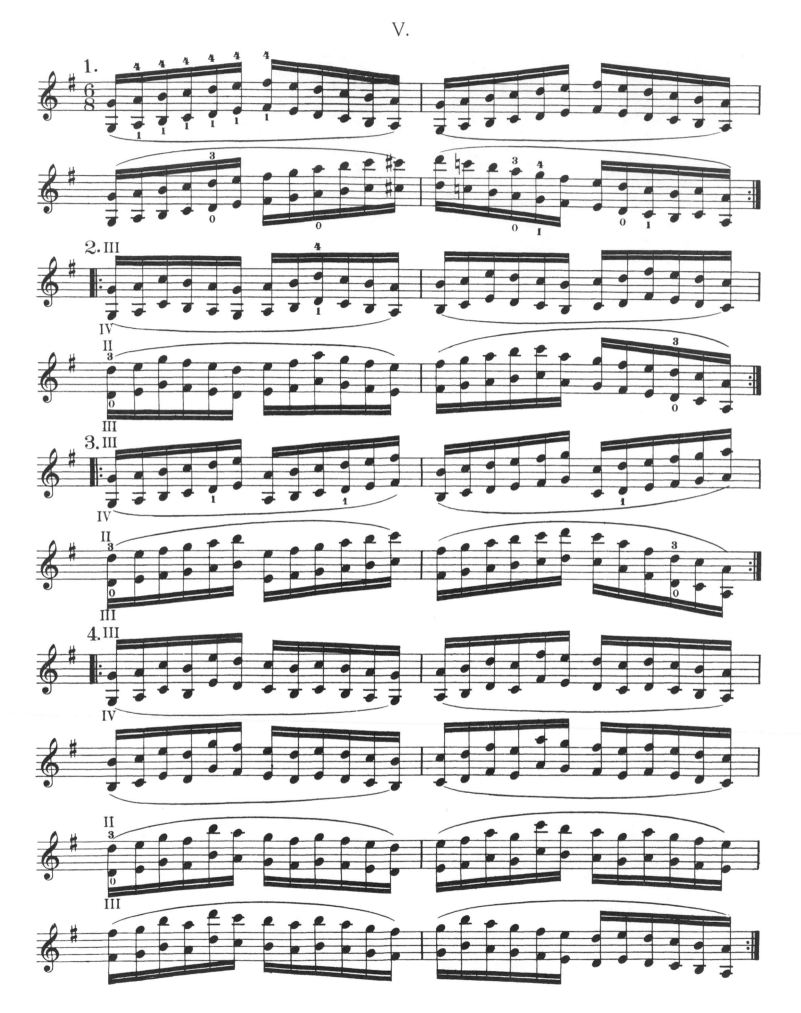

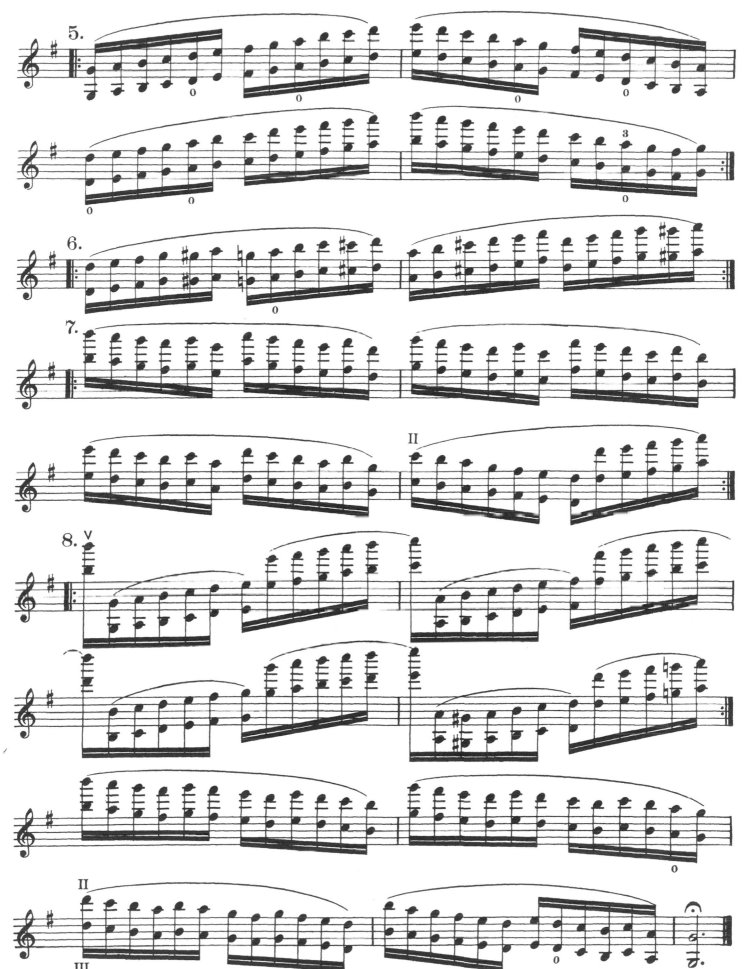

VII.

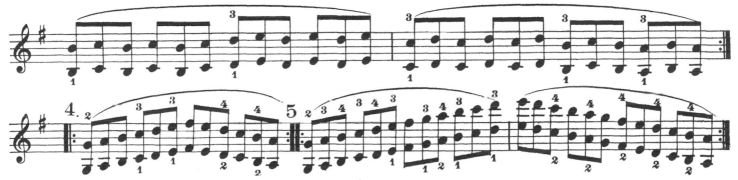

VIII.

IX.

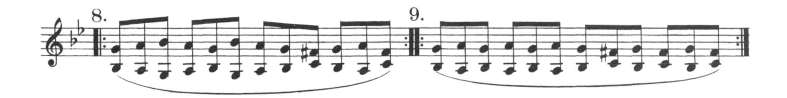

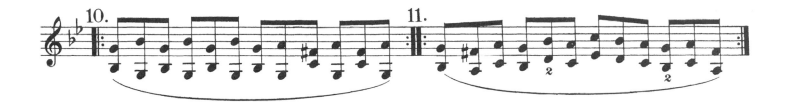

X.

The School of Violin-Technics
Book III*
Exercises in Various Bowings

I.

Henry Schradieck
(1846–1918)

* See pages 124–125 for Preface to Book III.

II.

III.

IV.

V.

VII.

VIII.

IX.

X.

XI.

XII.

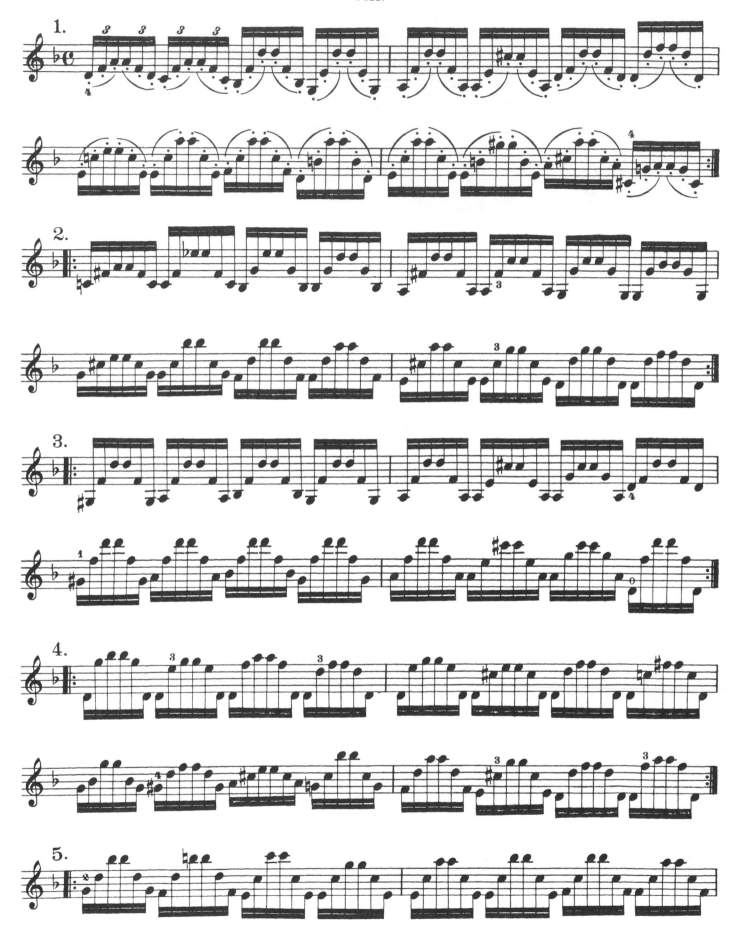

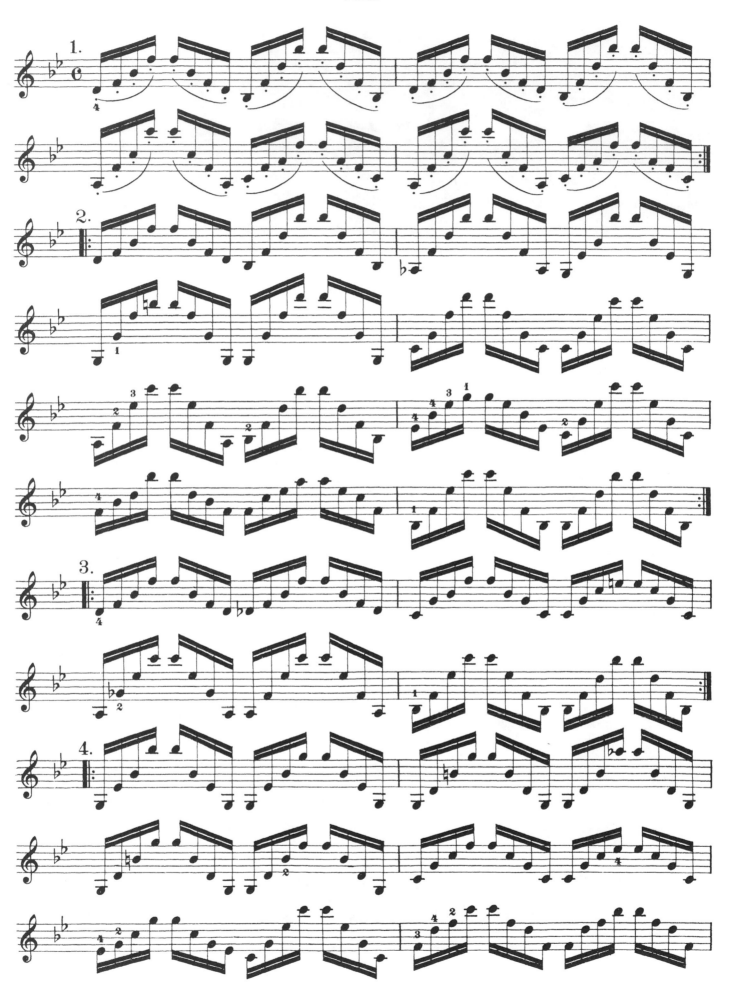

XIV.

XV.

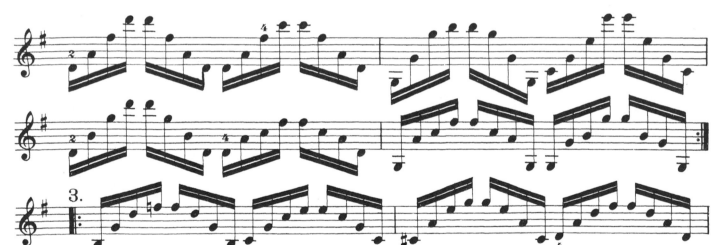

XVI.

(This page has intentionally been left blank.)

Complete Scale-Studies

I. Scales within the limits of One Position

Play every scale twice, and *without stopping* continue with the next one, as demonstrated in the first four lines. When the minor scale is played the second time, make in descending the change indicated in the 2nd and 4th line. Do not alternate with the fingering. First play all the scales in succession, beginning with the first finger, and then repeat them from B major, beginning with the second finger.

Henry Schradieck
(1846–1918)

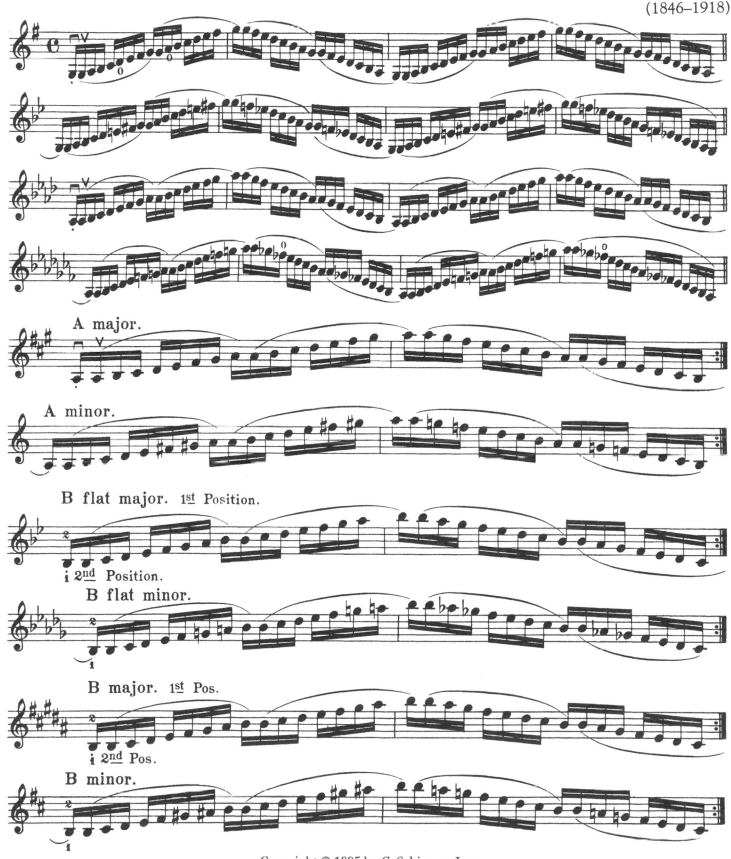

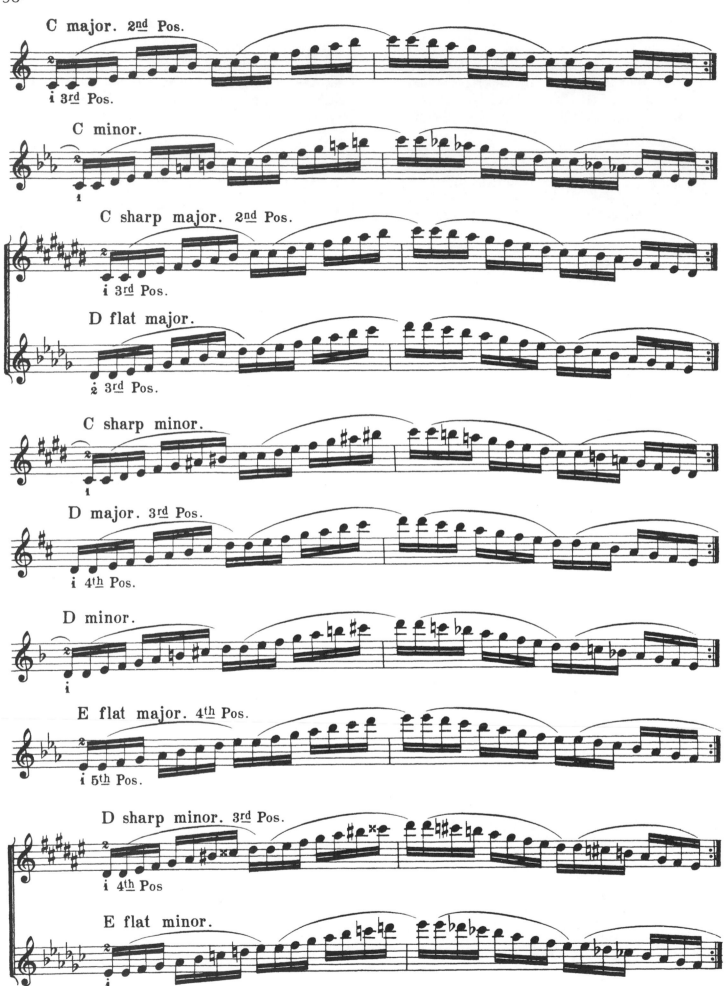

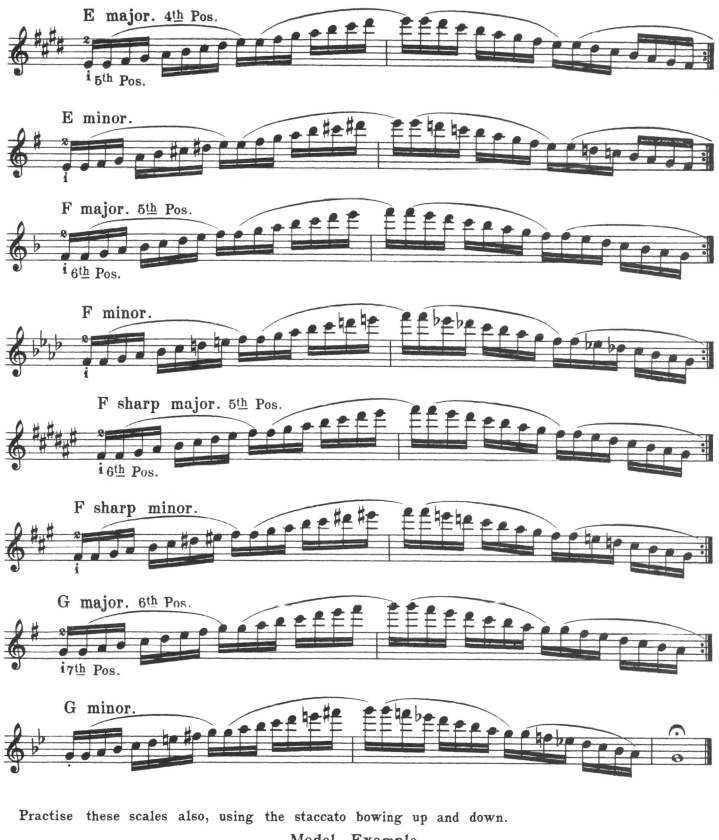

E major. 4th Pos.
5th Pos.

E minor.

F major. 5th Pos.
6th Pos.

F minor.

F sharp major. 5th Pos.
6th Pos.

F sharp minor.

G major. 6th Pos.
7th Pos.

G minor.

Practise these scales also, using the staccato bowing up and down.

Model Example.

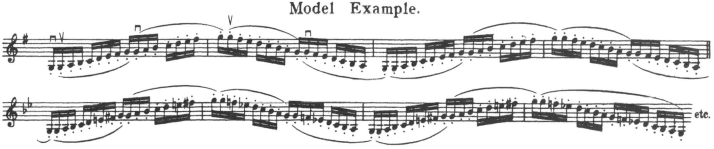

etc.

II. Scales with the omission of One Position

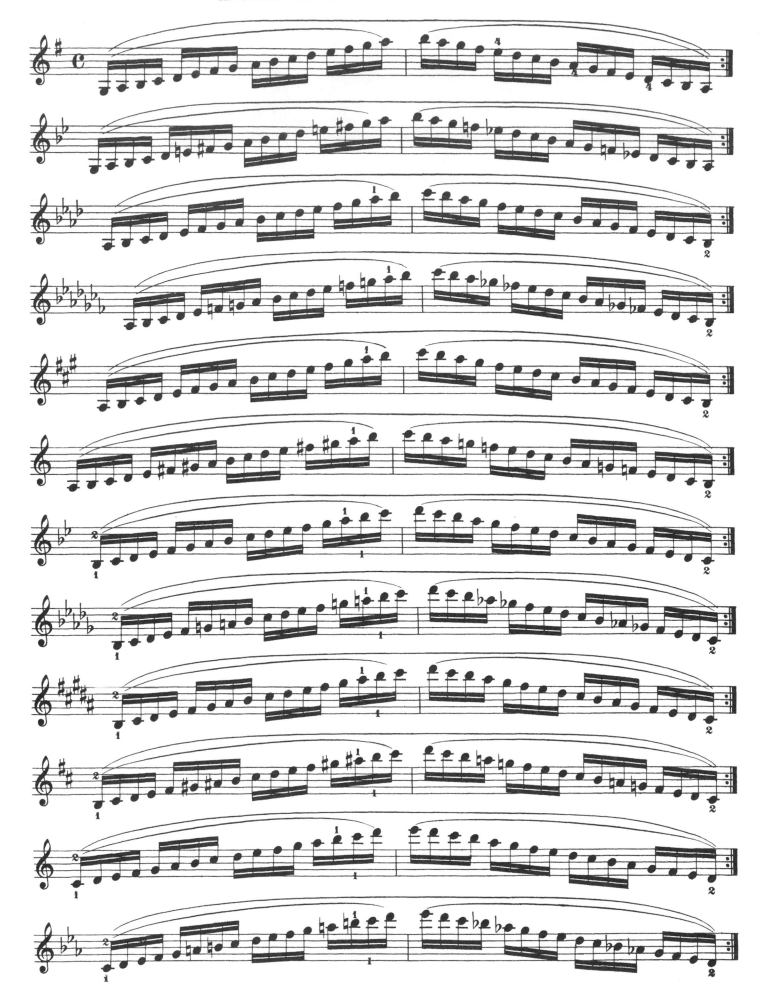

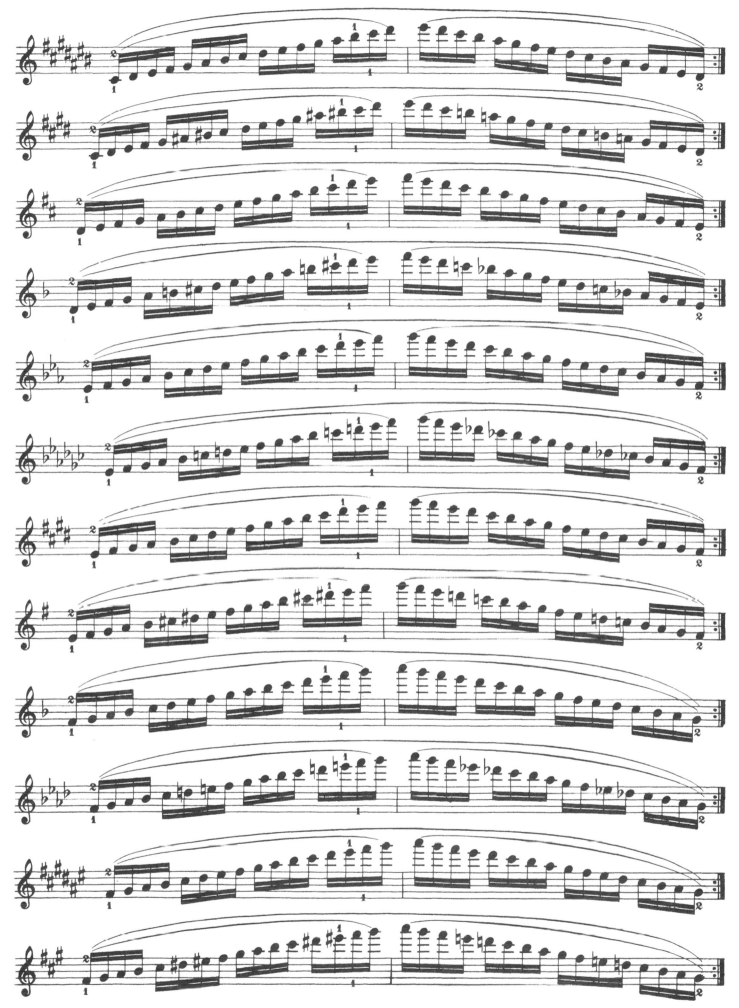

III. Harmonic minor scales in One Position

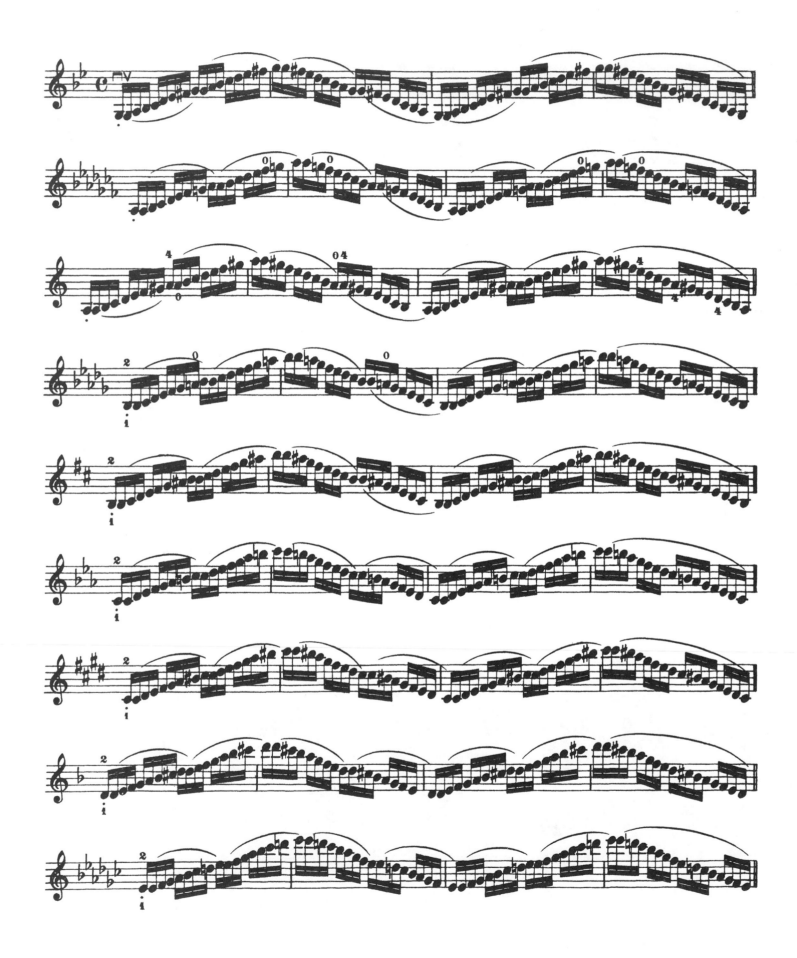

IV. Major and minor (Melodic and Harmonic) Scales
Through Three Octaves

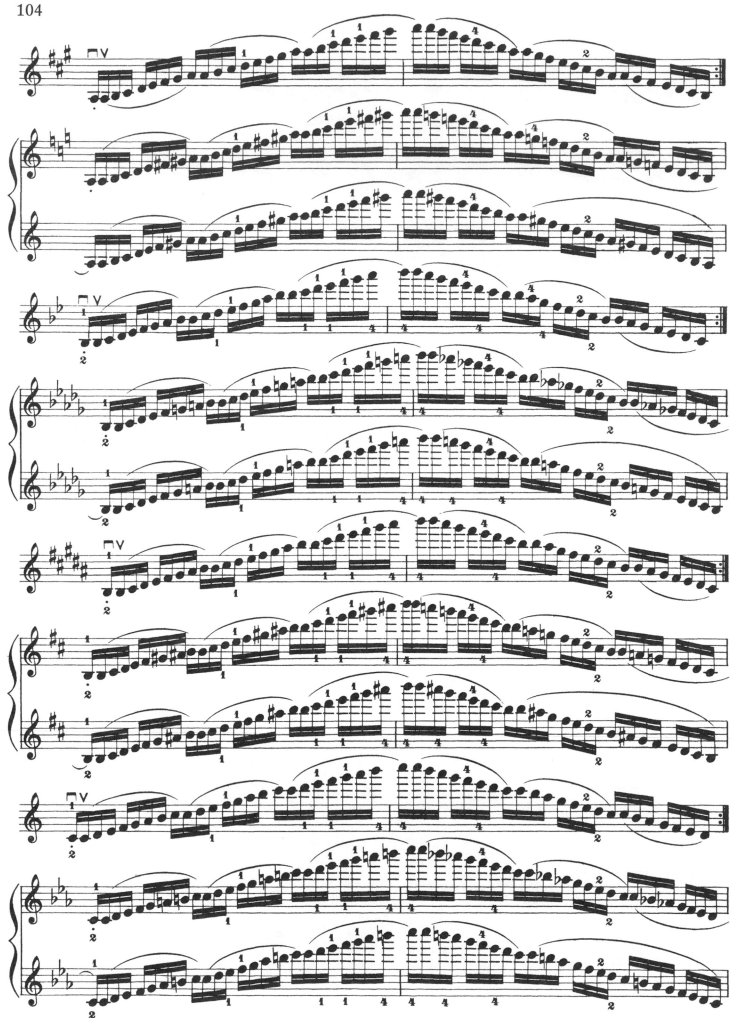

Also practise the scales under II, III and IV with the *staccato* bowing.

V. Scales through the Keys, in the Circle of Fifths

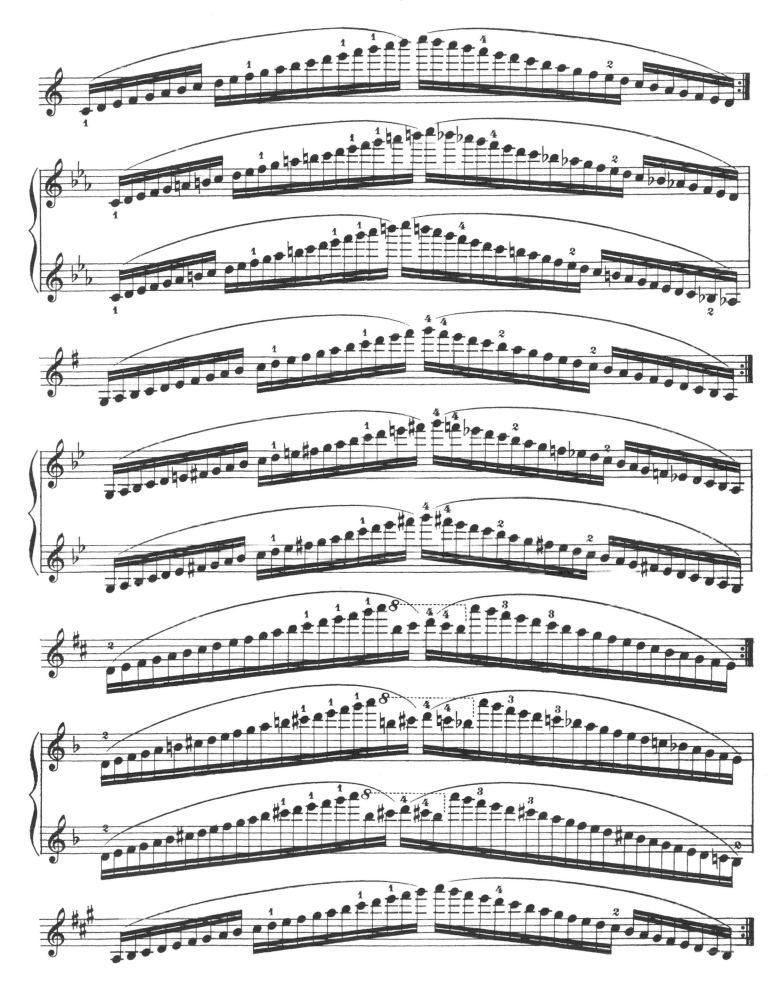

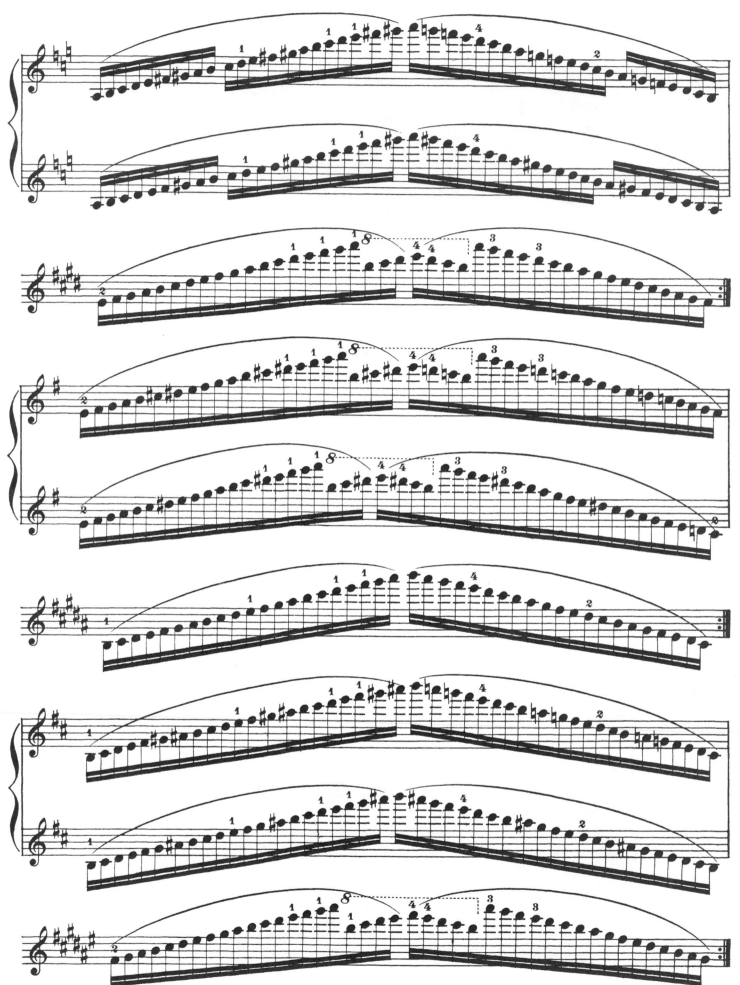

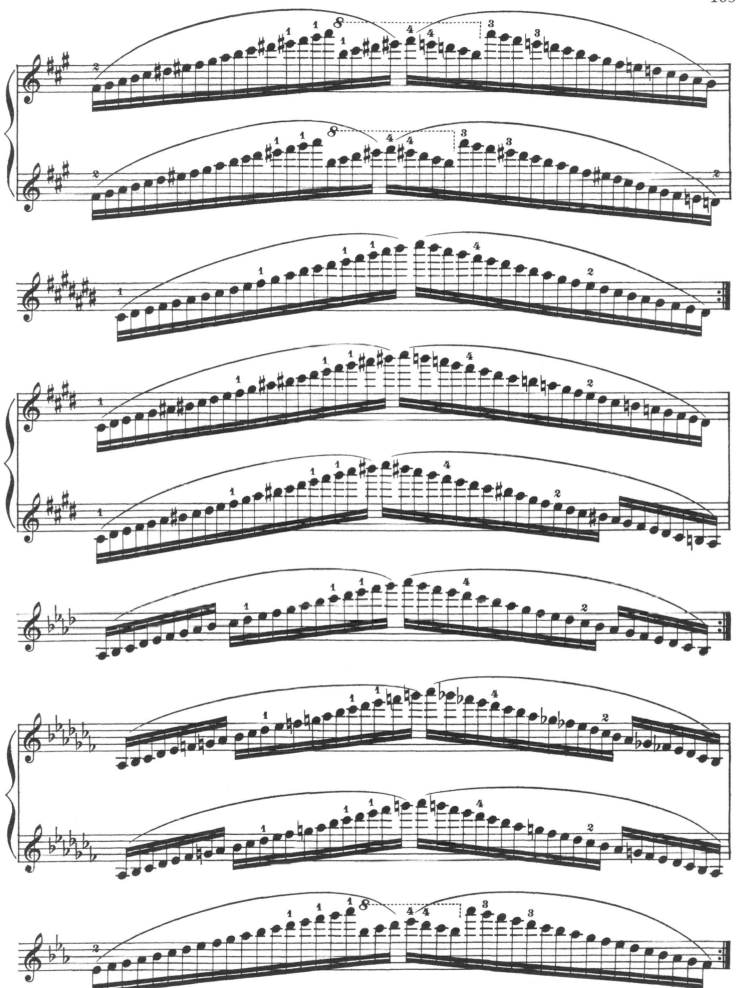

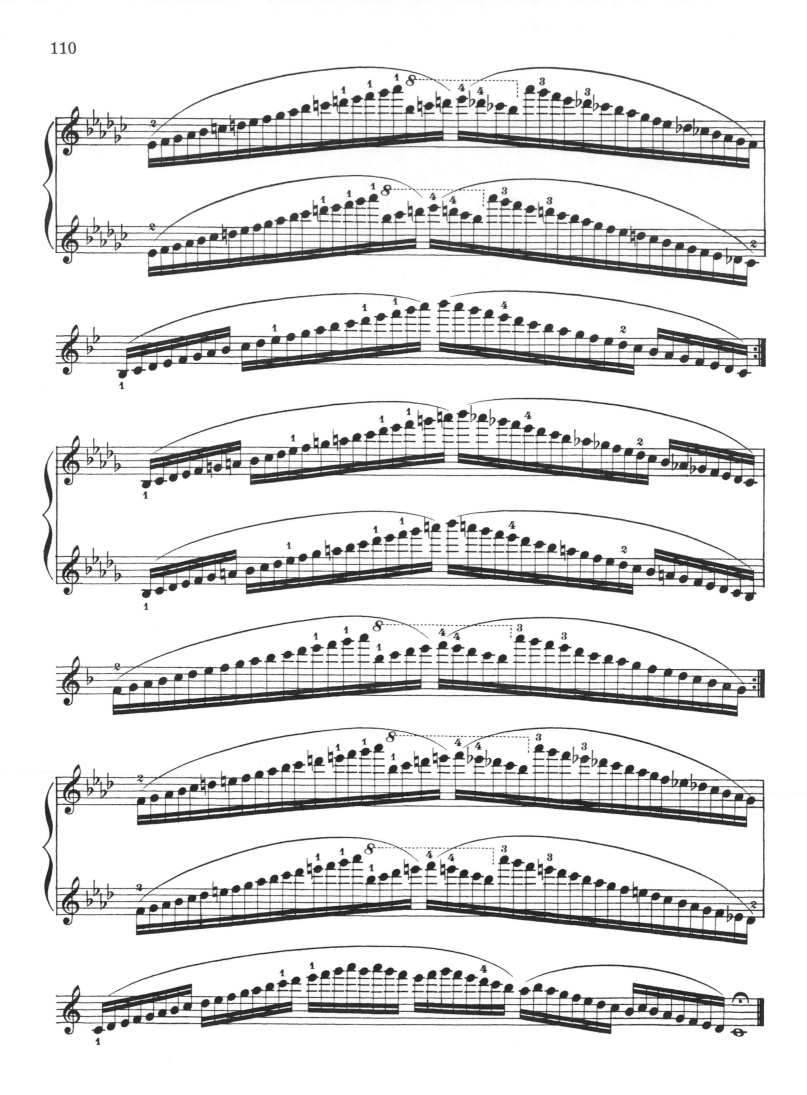

VI. Chromatic Scales in One Position

VII. Chromatic Scales through Three Octaves

From the 2nd Position.

From the 1st Position.

2nd Pos.

1st Pos.

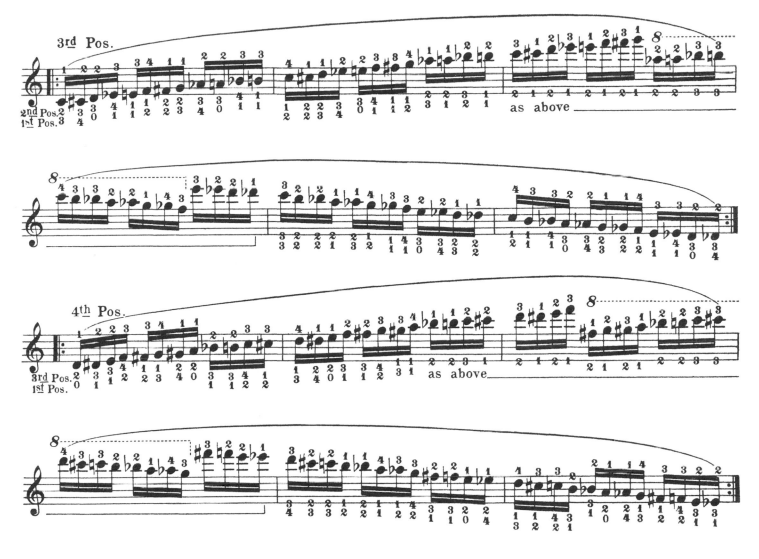

VIII. Scales in Octaves

Practise the scales in Octaves, as shown in the Model Examples below.

With the full bow and very short.

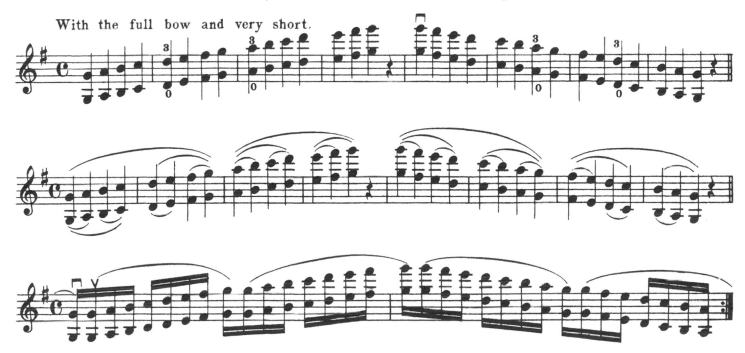

114

*) The fingering ⁴⁄₁ always indicates a change of string.

IX. Scales in Thirds

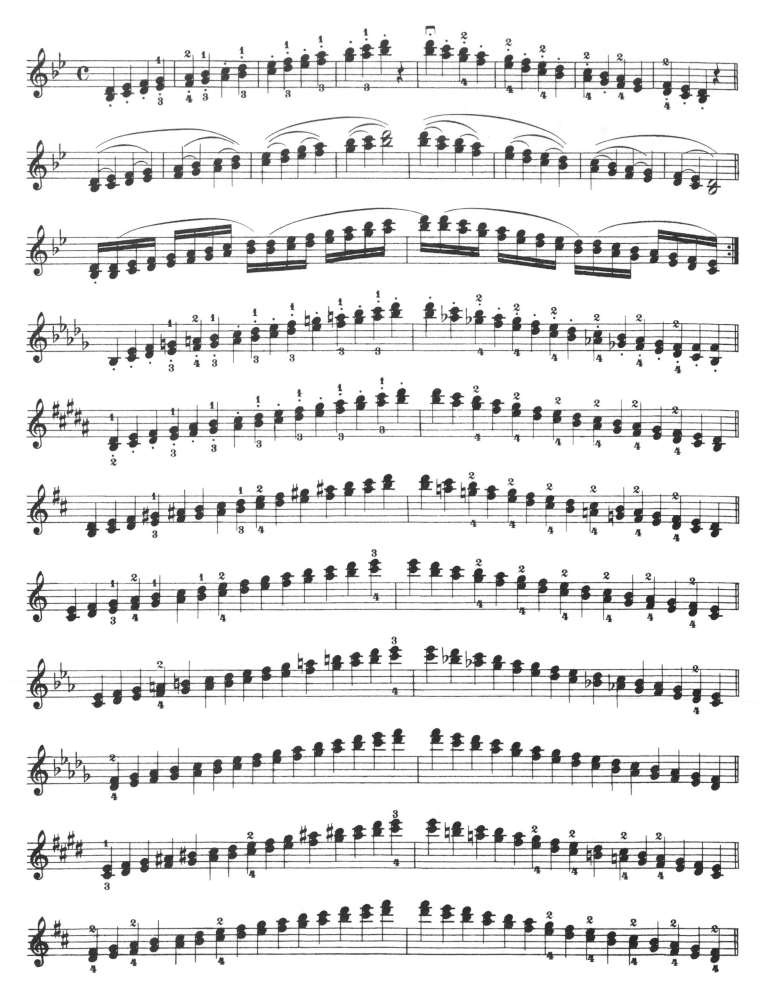

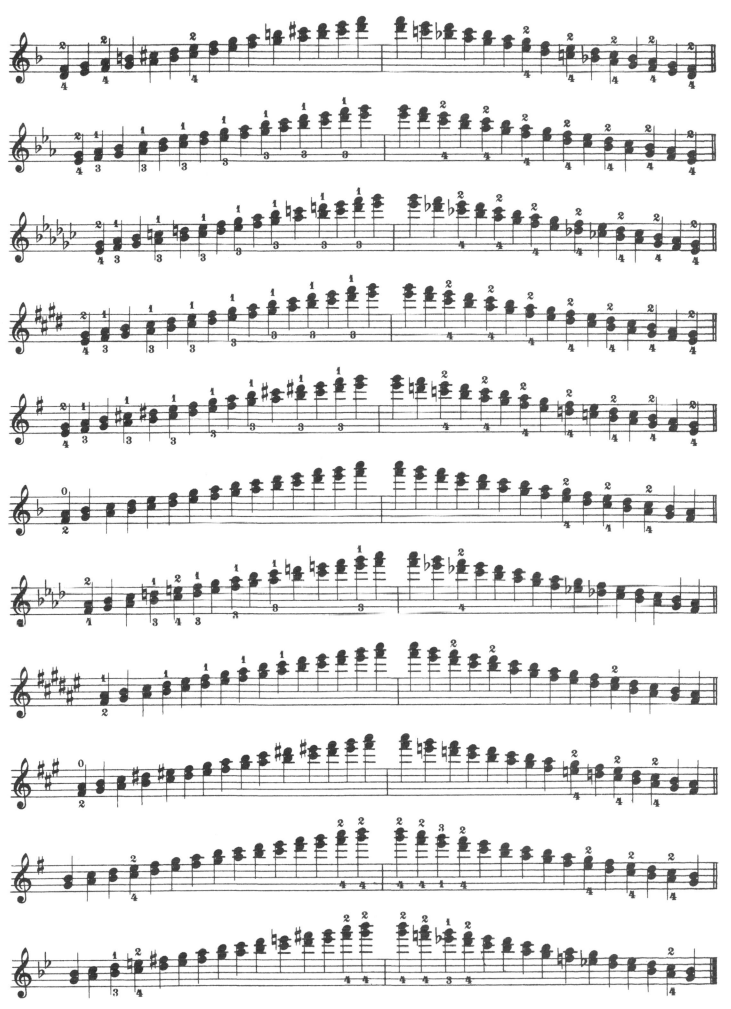

X. Scales in Thirds
Through the Circle of Fifths

XI. Scales in Sixths

These should be studied according to the Model Examples given on Page 113 for the Octaves and Thirds.

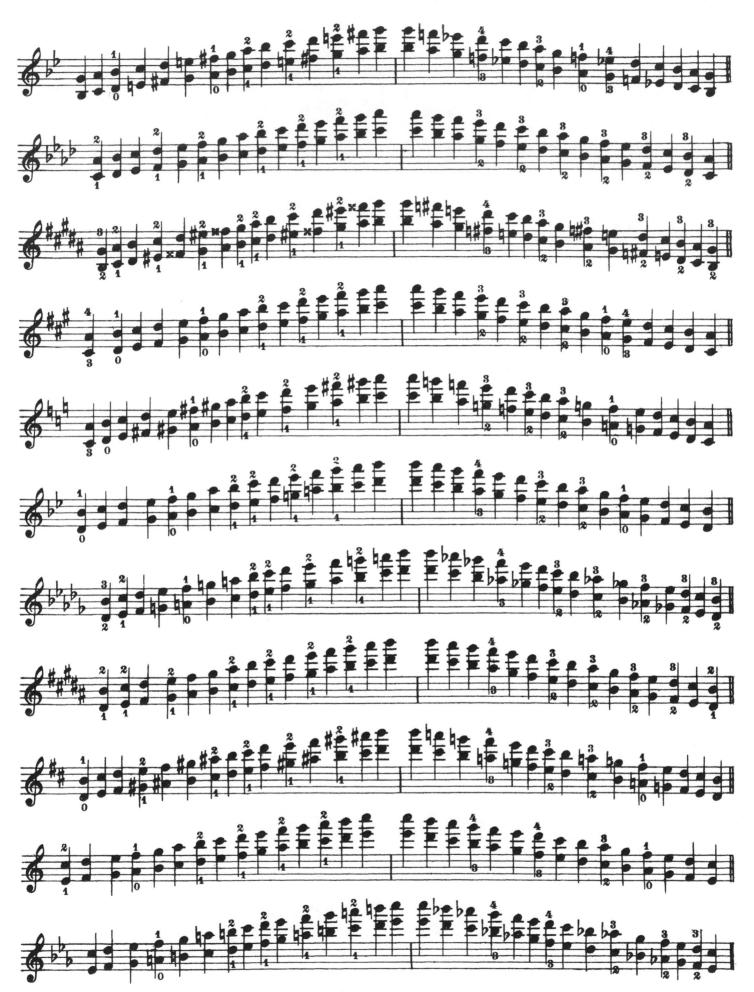

XII. A few Scales in Tenths

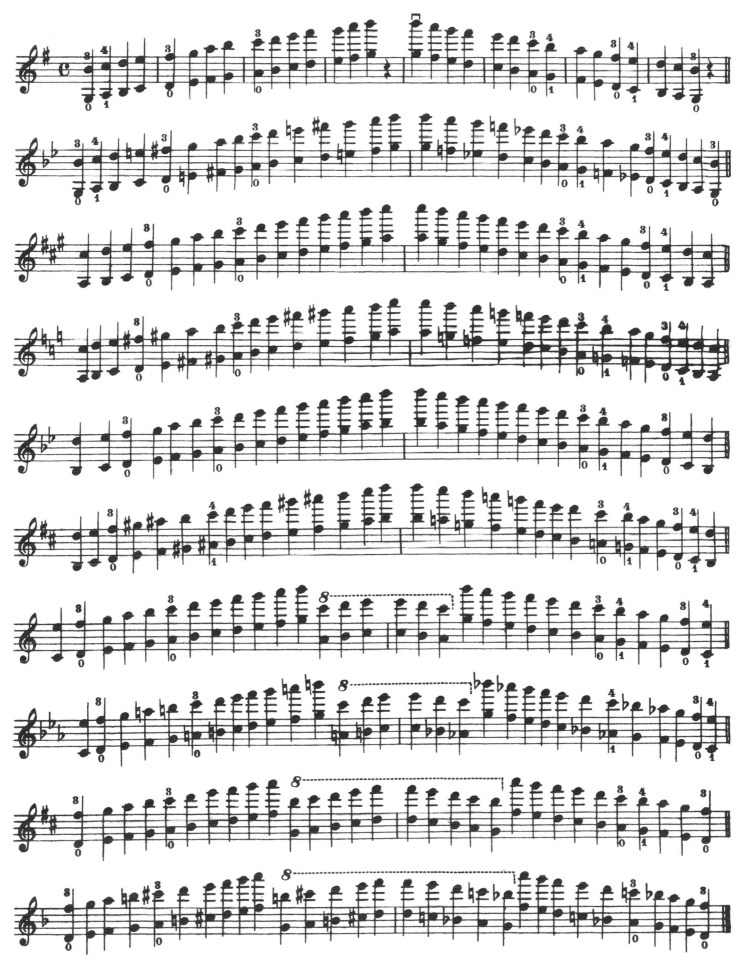

In Book III of this revised edition the author has made some changes, a number of styles of bowing having been added which were not included in the former edition.

The first seven sections (I to VII) contain chiefly exercises on the staccato. In the remainder, excepting the last (N? XVII) the bowings which are to be executed with springing bow are treated (*spiccato* arpeggios).

In order to acquire a good staccato, special attention must be paid to strengthening the arm-muscles. The violin-player should not neglect to strengthen his arms by daily gymnastic exercises. The best preliminary exercise for the staccato is the detached wrist-stroke, which should be executed quite near the point of the bow. Each note must be firmly attacked, but without stiffening the wrist in the least. By this stroke all the muscles chiefly concerned in producing the staccato are strengthened in no common degree. — Practise in this manner all exercises in Section II; e. g.,

As one of the best studies for this bowing, the E major Caprice by Rode should be noted here (N? IX).

The broad detached stroke has a peculiarly strengthening effect on the muscles of the forearm. This stroke is executed between middle and point of bow, with the forearm alone. The upper arm should not move at all; consequently, the elbow-joint must be perfectly loose. Avoid perceptible breaks between the tones. For the study of this stroke, all exercises in Nos. I, III, and

V may be utilized; e. g.,

Also practise Studies VIII and X (in F♯ minor and C♯ minor) of the Rode Caprices with this stroke.

The exercises in Nos. I, II, III and V are marked with two bowings. The best way to practise them is as follows:

(1) Employ only the bowing marked above.

(2) Employ only the bowing marked below.

(3) Employ, for each individual exercise, at first the upper bowing, and on repetition the lower bowing.

It will also be very helpful to play all the exercises in any section throughout with any one of the given bowings. As so many different bowings are indicated, the student will have to make a suitable selection.

The Springing Bow (*spiccato*) forms the foundation of all bowings to be executed with a "jumping" bow. This bowing cannot be practised too much; it is, therefore strongly recommended to utilize the entire contents of this Book as material for the practice of this bowing.

The *spiccato* (and, for that matter, all bowings executed with a "jumping" bow) is executed with a perfectly loose wrist about the middle of the bow, near the centre of gravity of the stick. This centre of gravity can be readily found by balancing the bow across the back of the violin; as a guide for the eye, the exact point may be marked with chalk.

It will also be very useful to the pupil to practise the exercises in Sections IX to XV in the following manner:

To N? IX.

To N? X.

To N? XI.

Also practise legato, with a perfectly loose wrist.

N?S 6, 9 and 10 must then be varied as follows; e. g.,

To Nº XII.

It is also excellent practice to play this section legato:

To Nº XIII.

Various chords in this section being difficult to stop, it is advisable to practise it at first as follows:

To Nº XVI.
At the point.